Sex And Sushi

TASSA DESALADA

Copyright © 2016 Tassa DeSalada

All rights reserved.

ISBN-10: 1537069357

ISBN-13: 978-1537069357

CONTENTS

	Introduction	i
1	Sex and Sushi	1
2	Saturday Night	13
3	Vices	19
4	Strong Feelings	29
5	Full Bush	37
6	Chocolate Anniversary	41
7	Sushi and Sex	46
8	The Kickstarter	53
9	Texts	64
10	The Alarm Clock	70

INTRODUCTION

This book is written in the first person by me…the woman…the wife. I love to fuck my husband. I love to have sex with him. He's the best. I feel all sorts of feelings and think all kinds of thoughts before, during, and after sex with my husband. Since I don't communicate well verbally, I write down my impressions and memories of our sex sessions, and then share them with my husband. He loves to read my accounts, and looks forward to getting them as a sort of post-coitus celebration. In this fashion, I'm able to express myself sexually. I'm able to communicate to him my innermost sexual thoughts and feelings, which I'm otherwise unable to do. These narratives have become habit forming for both of us and we both look forward to reading them. He likes them in order to read my "review" and I like them because I get to relive the most sensual moments of my life over and over again. It's thrilling and amazing at the same time. At a certain point, I realized that I had generated a nice collection of these "sessions" as I call them. I decided to compile these sessions into this book, which I hope you will enjoy.

1 SEX AND SUSHI

It's been a really long time since our last sex session, and I miss it sooooo much!!! He tells me he needs to spend time alone with me. That sounds promising. He sends the kids off to a babysitter's house giving us the luxury of privacy. That sounds really promising. I'm very willing to work this opportunity to its full potential. He leads me into our bedroom, and undresses me. I'm absolutely nude, from my nose to my toes. I try to undress him, but he takes the lead in undressing himself. He invites me to lay on the bed, butt up, face down. He tells me he wants to give me an anal orgasm. Wow!!! I melt just listening to that idea!! That can get messy. I tell him we need to put something on the bed to keep it clean. He gets a bath towel and spreads it on the bed. That's a good idea, but I wanted a super soft blanket so it would feel nice on my skin, and his skin. After all, every single sensation adds to the whole experience. That experience may as well include a nice soft blanket. I go get a blanket, and he gets the tub of lube from the bathroom.

He wants to start by giving me a back massage. He pats the bed with his right hand, and asks me to lay down on my tummy, butt up. I'm lovin' this. Of course I oblige. Why wouldn't I? I've been waiting for this extended session for weeks. I climb onto the bed, and wrap my arms around a scrawny pillow. I only want something to hold on to. I don't want a full pillow under my head to bend my back backwards. That wouldn't be comfortable. He straddles my ass and pours baby oil from my left shoulder to my right shoulder. OOOOoooooooh!!!!! He puts the bottle on the window sill, and starts massaging my upper back with both hands. He pays extra attention to my neck because for some reason it's been hurting me lately. I don't know how it became injured, but I'm glad it's getting the extra attention. It makes my neck feel much better. He grabs the bottle from the sill, and spills more oil on my back. But this time, the spill creates an interesting path starting at the spot directly between my upper shoulders, down my backbone, and zigzags across the top of my butt crack. I like where he's going with this. He places the bottle back on the sill, and starts massaging the oil into my skin. He starts at the spot between my shoulders, and works his hands out from my backbone towards my sides. I'm excitedly waiting for him to approach the top of my butt and work my ass. Eventually he does so, but he takes his time and makes me wait. He doesn't know he's making me wait. I can't let him on to that fact, because then he'll make me wait even longer. The anticipation is creating tingles along my backbone where his hands roam freely, firmly, and slowly. Finally, he shimmies his body down my legs, and his hands start to massage the top of my crack. I don't know why it is, but that spot feels fantastic when he's massaging it. It's as if it's the doorbell to the gates of my pleasure. It's not a flood of pleasure, but it's enough to get my full attention, and to put a big smile of my face. I can start to think about how good this spot feels, and that makes it feel even better. It only needs the slightest suggestion, and the feeling can start to relax my entire ass. He grabs a cheek in each hand and very lovingly squeezes each cheek. My ass cheeks tighten to meet his hands. Am I slightly sticking my ass up to help him go deeper with the massage? Maybe. I'm not sure. But that would make sense. He rubs his finger over each cheek in a deep circular motion. OOOOoooooooohh!!! He's hitting all the right spots!!! He tells me I have the nicest ass he's ever seen. He tells me it's perfect in every which way, outside and inside. If only I could live like this, every day, all day. I would need a portable butt massager, but that would do the job without the love. I want the love. It adds a whole new dimension to the feeling. He unstraddles me, and pours more oil down each of my legs. I can feel the oil drip down the side of each leg before he has a chance to massage the oil into my skin. I wish he would have spent more time on the butt, but if it were up to me, I'd love a never-ending butt massage. Of course, that would not end with an orgasm, and I want that orgasm. So I go with the flow. The leg massage is nice too.

He asks me to flip over onto my back. I eagerly flip over. He says he wants to work my clitoris. Ok, my legs spread open. He searches thru our basket of lubes and finds the KY Jelly. He says that'll be good enough. He gets himself into position with his face between my legs. He smells my box. He says he just loves my scent. It smells wonderful. He luxuriates in the experience, with an arm around each of my legs. He takes a break and squirts lube on the tips of his two front fingers. His two fingers find my clitoris, and roll around the base of my clitoris. Somehow his thumb also gets in on the action. He gently spreads the pussy lips with his fingers, and ever so slowly pulls on my clitoris with his lips. It's as if he's stroking off my miniature penis. Whatever he's doing, it feels fantastic. I tell him so. His tongue thoroughly works my clitoris. It touches the tip of the clitoris, then it circles the clitoris until it gets down to its base. My clitoris is small, but the sensations he's giving me are absolutely huge!! His lips suck on my clitoris. He kisses it too. His tongue wiggles its way down towards my lips and caresses them, gently and lovingly, and slowly, and warmly, up and down. Eventually he uses his hands to push my legs up and roll me back. This gives him easier access to my asshole.

He keeps his hands under my knees to make sure my legs stay up. He kisses my asshole, and lightly sucks on it. The sucking gets stronger and stronger. This feels so fantastic!!! His tongue rims my asshole, and finds its way inside my asshole. He's tongue-fucking my asshole! OOOOoooooohhh!!! I'm in heaven!! His tongue searches inside for something, and then plunges in and out. Yikes!!! I wish his tongue were longer. But it doesn't matter. It's a roll-my-eyes-into-the-back-of-my-head pleasure. I can go berserk with this feeling. He pulls his tongue out, but I don't notice. My mind is racing with pleasure. My ass feels fantastic!!

He squirts more lube on my asshole, and on his fingers. He starts tonguing my clitoris again. He starts to stroke my asshole with the tips of his fingers. Holy shit!! The combination is electrifying. I moan and groan loudly. I try to grab something with my pussy, to try and pull it into my pussy. A finger or a tongue would do very, very nicely. But no such luck. The clitoris and the butt get all the attention. Pussy gets starved. But that doesn't mean she can't work whatever she has. She pulls on the inside. She grabs, but has nothing to grab. His finger enters my asshole. Woweee!!! The electric feeling just got electrified. The combination of the sucking of the clitoris and the finger up my ass is absolutely incredible!!! Forget about the pussy. My asshole has something solid with which to work. And he's still tonguing the clitoris!!! Something amazing is going to happen. I'm well on my way. I just need to work my insides. My clitoris is going berserk from all the sucking. But for some reason it wants to be massaged from inside my asshole. If only I can suck that finger up my asshole, and massage my clitoris, that would surely be an anal orgasm, or some kind of orgasm. If a woman has an orgasm, then she should consider herself lucky. If a woman has an anal orgasm, then she is lucky indeed. I believe I'm on my way to a fantastic anal orgasm, with many thanks to my wonderful husband. I'm fully set up. My husband's tonguing my clitoris, and has his finger stuck up my asshole. Now I have to put in lots of time, and effort. I know I can do it. I want that orgasm!!! That finger's coming inside!! I pull, and pull, and pull. I pull my outer ass muscles towards my insides because that's where I want his finger to go. I pull with all of my might, but it's not coming in any further. He's holding back on me!!! This makes me go crazy. I have to work every ass muscle that I have. I know I can do this. I work my inside ass muscles. I work my deeper inside ass muscles. I work my sphincter circular asshole muscle to grab his finger. I move my legs around, maybe that'll help. I firmly set my hands on the bed, and try to pull his finger by grabbing onto his finger, and pulling my entire body away from him. Nothing. No success. Ugh!! Something's gotta work. He places two fingers inside my asshole. I can really feel the difference! And I love it!!! Now I have more substance to grab onto, and to pull inside. I clamp down with my sphincter muscle, and get a really good hold of his fingers. I'm sure that works. I use my inner muscles to try to pull them inside. For some reason, the fingers are staying still. I try and I try. I pull and I pull. My actions really escalate the great feelings inside of me. I know if I keep trying, I will eventually reach that cliff, and blissfully fall over it. Oh!! I can't wait!! I need to keep trying my hardest!! He gently opens his fingers inside my asshole to create a scissor action and opens and closes his index and middle fingers. He's inserted just his two fingers, up to the second knuckle. The scissor action stops my asshole sphincter muscle from closing during one of its grab sessions. He says it takes a lot of strength to counteract that strong ass muscle, but that's the resistance that gives me an anal orgasm. I'm engaging every butt muscle I have in order to pull on those fingers, and rub my clitoris from the inside. I'm sure that's what I want. I'm using my Gluteus Maximus outer muscles. I'm using my inner butt muscles. With each try, I get a stronger taste of the upcoming orgasm, so long as I put in my all-out effort. I want that feeling so bad!!! It's a slightly delayed pleasure. I grab, and can't help but release after a certain length of time. Only after the release do I start to feel hyper intense pleasure. It's not long, maybe a couple seconds or so. I'm sure if I could sustain the grab for a longer time period, then the grab time would overlap with the pleasure time. That would self-perpetuate those fantastic feelings. For some reason, that's too hard for me to do. I've heard that once the human orgasm starts, there's no stopping it. But I need to get to that point. I need to get my orgasm started. And I'm not there yet. One more, strong try. I grab on to the scissor fingers. I give it my all. I know I need to grab with all of my might to get the orgasm started. I grab those fingers with every muscle I've got. And I get everything in return. The orgasm's starting. I know I need to grab for as long as I can to extend the orgasm as much as possible. I know I can only grab for so long before the pleasure takes over, and I give in to it, thus letting go of my vice grip.

That much pleasure will loosen anyone's grip on anything. The cliff is in view. OOOooooooooooohhhh!!!! I'm going over that cliff!!! My brain is soaking up that fantastic feeling like a dry sponge in the desert. The pleasures are too strong for me to keep my ass hold any longer. So I start to relax my ass muscles. I'm taken to another dimension to ride out this pleasure wave. I'm still inside my body, but my brain has expanded a hundred-fold in order to fully engulf all of the pleasures it's feeling right now. It's exploding with pleasure. Fireworks are going off in all directions, sparking all sorts of ooooooohhhhhs and aaaaaaaaaahhhhs from me. That's clearly a Russian Feather Orgasm. No doubt about it. The feelings begin to subside, and I'm extremely happy. My husband is still massaging my butthole. He's still plunging his fingers in and out of my asshole, as deep as he can go. He says my hole opened up, but now it's starting to settle back down to normal size again. The ass muscles really clamp down on his fingers. The key to my pleasures is for him to play with my asshole. I didn't realize my asshole had much playing potential, but I'm so glad that he's able to tap into it. His fingers are still playing with my ass. I like that. I know the other times I've simply rolled over, and been done. But, for some reason, that didn't happen this time.

He thinks I'm done after that fantastic anal orgasm. The satisfied butt is the key to my happiness. But, uh, no, I'm not done. My ass is pretty much fried, but it's been too long. I'm too starved to let this opportunity pass without fully milking it. My pussy wants sex. I also want to feel him blow his load inside of me.

He agrees. We decide to do it missionary style, in the pussy. We need to give pussy some attention since she's been overlooked so far. It's nice to have these options available. I take his dick in my hands, and start to roll it around between my palms, and if I were rolling out a pretzel. He squirts lots of KY on his dick. He says it feels much better that way. I agree. I know lube feels much better for me than no lube. My pussy's not dry, but lube is lube, and sex feels much better with lots of lube. I grab dickie with my left hand, and pump him with an emphasis on pulling. My right hand reaches between his legs, and massages his balls. They're swollen, and full. Dickie is hard. He's ready. And he tells me so. I grab a washcloth to wipe my dripping hands. I lean back on the bed, and spread my legs to receive him. He positions himself between my legs, and guides dickie inside my pussy. I'm lovin' this!! I can't believe I'm having pussy sex after I've just had a full-blown anal orgasm. The feeling is extra sensational. My private area is still burning with pleasure from the anal orgasm. The pussy's the only part that's been neglected. The pussy's been in the center of it because it's located between the clitoris and the ass. Now everything will have gotten special attention. Dickie enters pussy very slowly, and very gently. I always love to fuck, and especially this time. My pussy must have tons of pleasure points inside of it. When dickie starts his way inside, then my brain is on pleasure overload. He goes all-in. I can feel the balls pressing against my ass – another fantastic sensation!!! This stirs up the feelings of the anal orgasm. Yikes!!! He starts pumping in and out. As each thrust enters me, and finds its way to its deepest length, the pressures gradually build and intensify. As the speed increases, the pressures and the pleasures come more often. Dickie is still growing in length, and girth, and stiffness. This increases the pressures, and thus, the pleasures of my insides. More pressure over a larger area creates lots more pleasure. Add a strong dose of love, and eventually the pressures build the pleasures to such an intensity that my mind goes on overload. That's a really intense pussy fuck!!! I love to fuck!! He looks into my eyes, and smiles. I smile back. I love that. I keep telling him I love to fuck. I wish I could vary that comment in any way. But those same words keep coming out of my mouth. I hope he knows I mean so much more. I just can't think of anything else to say. And that's the truth!! He's pumping, and I decide to add a little variety. I grab dickie with pussy. This feels fantastic in its own right. It's somehow reminiscent of my ass grabbing his scissor fingers, except it's sourced in the pussy. Somehow something works in that effort. I grab him as he pulls out. I try to pull him back in, as he pulls out. I loosen the muscles when he pushes in. I don't want anything to get in the way of his coming inside of me, not for a split second. I try to synchronize my grabbing with his pumping, but I'm not always at the same speed. It's hard to control those pussy muscles and combine them with pumping actions. It's even harder to match a very specific rhythm. But I keep trying, because I love to fuck.

He's out of breath. I certainly don't want him to overexert himself, so I suggest that we try doggie style with me bending over the edge of the bed, and our feet are on the ground. Maybe that would be easier. He agrees. I take off my socks because I know that my feet will need to have good traction on the bare wood floor. We position ourselves, and dickie visits pussy again. I try to move my butt up and down to find the right height. This feels so fantastic that I melt into the bed. The left side of my face is smothered in the blanket, and my arms are stretched out to the sides. I love to fuck. He grabs my hips with his hands and starts to pump. I try to match the rhythm while trying to pump and grab. That's way too much for me to do, so I just try to pump. Dickie's big by now, so it's hard to grab him anyway. It feels so much better when I try to slam him. We go pretty fast. The feelings are fantastic!! The pleasure becomes much more intense. The pumping, the slamming, the deepness, the double use of my ass and pussy. It all adds up to fantastic sex. I'm bending over the bed. My arms fall down the side of the bed at a right angle to give me the support I need to pump him while he's pumping me. Things are getting pretty wild. I love the deepness. I'm also beginning to feel his size getting bigger, and bigger, and bigger. I find myself screaming from the pleasure. I know he's fully loaded, and I tell him to blow. He says OK, and pumps even harder. He grabs my hair, and pulls my head back. I love to fuck. He cums, and things slow down. He pulls out. I fall into the bed, and invite him to join me. He does so, and we talk about lots of things. He invites me to a sushi lunch with him. I gratefully accept. After all, that's my ideal date – sex and sushi. I just love it.

We walk into the sushi restaurant, and get seated right away. The sushi chef looks at me, and smiles. I smile back. I wonder if he knows what we've been doing. Is it obvious? I can't tell. I glance around the restaurant. There are several other couples in the restaurant. They're really dressed down. From the looks on their faces, they look like they've just had sex, just like us. It looks like this is the place to go to after you've had your Saturday noontime sex. However, I can also tell by the looks on their faces that they didn't have the amazing orgasms like I did. I feel sorry for them. I'm the most fucked-out of all these people. That much is clear. Maybe they need to try anal sex. Maybe then they'll look the way they want to look, like they've just had the biggest fucking orgasm of their life. You can't fake that look. It comes from way down deep inside. We order six long sushi rolls. That's too much food, but I'm starving. My husband really knows how to make the most of our time together – an anal orgasm, a pussy orgasm, and then a delicious sushi lunch. Somehow we finish all of the sushi, and leave with smiles on our faces.

2 SATURDAY NIGHT

Saturday night, 6pm

Since I can't remember everything that goes through my mind when I have an anal orgasm, I decide to type out my thoughts and feelings on my phone while my husband's working me over. There are times when I simply lose my mind, and I have to stop typing because the feelings are too intense. However, when I can type, I do. Following is the result of my Saturday Night anal orgasm experience.

We're cuddling in the bedroom. There are lots of hugs, kisses, lipsies on my mouth lips, and french kisses. His hands roam towards my butt, massaging all my body parts on the way down. My clitoris gets a full hand massage. It's really too small to get a full hand massage, but a full hand massage makes the clitoris feel that much better. ALL of it gets massaged. No part of the clitoris is left untouched. It's also much better than a single finger massage. I lay on the bed, on my back, and open my legs. He face dives my pussy. He loves my smell. He loves my taste. My inner thighs relax, and my legs open up even more. He's taking his time to enjoy my smell. He kisses my inner knees, thighs, pussy lips. There's that butthole he's been thinking about all day long. He says he couldn't stop thinking about it. His lips gently pull on my pussy's outer lips. His tongue slowly goes up and down my pussy lips. He massages my outer legs with the palms of his hands. He pulls on my pussy lips with his own lips, over and over, no place he'd rather be. There's no place I'd rather be. I'm relaxing, and there's a small orgasm inside my pussy. His tongue goes way inside my pussy, as far as it can go. Yay! He kisses the outside of my butthole, and my legs go up. He licks clitoris, gently opens my pussy lips with his fingers, and licks the inside of my pussy lips, again and again. He massages my buttocks with his hands. I close my eyes and enjoy, smiling. He licks the inside of my pussy lips. There's no place I'd rather be… there's no place I'd rather be. My legs go up involuntarily. My knees press on my shoulders. He rims my butthole with his tongue. He kisses my butthole. He massages my buttocks with his hands, then spreads my butthole, and kisses the inside of my butthole. His tongue goes inside. Oooooooooooohhhh! I'm really enjoying this! I'm groaning. He rims my butthole with his tongue, then sucks on my butthole. He massages my buttocks with his fingertips, but just outside the hole. He licks the area from the clitoris to the butthole, up and down, down and up, repeat. He gets up on his knees, squirts lube on his right hand, and spreads the lube on my clitoris. He squirts more lube on his hand, then spreads lube on my clitoris with his hand, and turns his butt towards me, alongside me. I grab his balls and buttcheeks. I massage his balls, and butt-cheeks. There's more relaxing, and massaging. His finger goes inside my pussy, and starts playing with my G spot. His fingers go in deeper, and start to swirl around. He has nice long fingers. His fingertip sways back and forth in the deep pussy. The other hand's fingers circle the butthole. Ecstasy! His fingers are deep in my pussy and swaying back and forth, searching and finding a pleasure spot. He slowly pulls his fingers out. I'm groaning. His left hand's working the clitoris, and his right hand's working my butthole. He flips me onto my tummy and massages my buttcheeks with both hands. He lays on me, his tummy on my back. I love it!!! He tells me he wants to put dickie in my butt, and instead massages my butt. He's teasing me!!! I'm groaning. He's massaging the top of my crack with his hand. He slowly pushes his body down my back. Now his face is at my ass. He spreads my buttcheeks with his hands, kisses the butthole, and tongue-rims my butthole. His tongue goes inside my butthole. Ecstasy! His tongue darts in-and-out of my butthole. I'm groaning. I can't stop groaning. Butt massage, thigh massage, boob massage. He places one finger in the butt, and shakes the finger around. He pulls his finger out, and covers it with lube. More lube, lots more lube. His fingers spread lube around my buttrim, then outside my butthole, then inside my butthole. Butthole has one finger inside. One finger starts to feel inadequate. The other hand massages my buttcheeks. I'm groaning, relaxing. He starts smaller massages on my ass, lays on me, his tummy on my back, and massages my butt. His finger's still inside my butthole. He massages the top of my crack, turns me over onto my back, and gives me a good butthole massage. There's the small shaking of his finger. He squirts lube on his hand, and spreads my legs. He puts his mouth on my pussy lips, rests his left hand on the inside of my left leg, and gently sticks his finger in my butt. Ecstasy! He sucks on my clitoris. I'm reaching from my insides, towards the clitoris. I keep reaching, going nuts, shaking, pulling with my butthole, pushing clitoris out, and rubbing my inside butt walls together, repeat. He now puts two fingers in-and-out of my butthole, and starts pumping the fingers in-and-out while sucking clitoris. I'm feeling the climax coming closer. This is insanity!!! Pussy feels an inside shove towards a small climax. His finger is gently yet firmly shaking in my ass, and a loud climax takes over me. I'm yelling loud. He's sucking on clitoris, while his fingers are still up my asshole. I'm groaning. His fingers are parked inside my butt, and his mouth is on my pussy.

Ahhhhhhhhhhhhhhhhhhhhhhhhhhhhhhhhhhhhhhhhhhhhhhh ! Total relaxation!!!!!! I wish I could feel this feeling forever!!!!! I feel butt pulling, and pushing, on my insides. Small tingles are fluttering all over my private area. He kisses the pussy lips. He tells me it was a Mapplethorpe moment. I couldn't see anything. I could only feel. I'm sure he's right. I agree. I thank him. He tells me if he had lube, it could've been a fist up there. That's the Mapplethorpe Moment – ass completely relaxed and wide open. He says butt pulls on his fingers with lots of force. It's hard for him to control all that pulling. I'm thanking him again and again. I'm sorry I'm typing. I had to stop typing in order to cum. It takes all my energy, and focus, and attention, and everything else of mine. He's massaging my buttocks. I show him my writing. He reads this piece and tells me it's great.

We're cleaning up now. Showering, washing our faces, brushing our teeth, putting on new clothes, throwing the old clothes in the laundry. I'm pulling up the blanket to throw it in the wash downstairs. He just complained that he did a rush job, and he doesn't feel as if he did a good job. I wholeheartedly disagree. He's sorry he has to wash off my smell. He tells me he smells like my hairy pussy. He does. He's right.

Hours later, I'm laying on the bed. My private area is feeling super good, and super relaxed. My pussy's relaxed. My ass's relaxed. My face is relaxed. My shoulders are relaxed. My legs are relaxed. Ok, I'm super relaxed all over. In fact, I'm a jellyfish! I just want to lay back and relax. This reminds me of the amazing interlude we had earlier. Wow! An anal orgasm on demand! Amazing! I'm fully worked over, relaxed, and very satisfied. I'm VERY, VERY happy. That's a great way to make a happy wife.

I keep reading the stuff above over and over and I can't believe that I wrote it! Moreover, I can't believe that I lived it! I can't believe that I experienced it! It's very hard to type during these intimate times. It's incredibly intrusive, and doesn't allow me to fully enjoy the moment. It's incredibly rude to my husband. However, this writing's incredible, and I love to read it over and over again. It heats me up even though I've read it hundreds of times. It keeps a memory of our most intimate moments alive and well inside our heads. Looking back, I simply would've remembered the incredible feelings, and not the play-by-play description. Whenever each of us reads this writing, it reminds us both of the fantastic event.

3 VICES

My husband and I are out to lunch. We're sitting across the table from each other. He looks around to see who's watching us, then looks right at me. He cups his hands around his lips, and mouths to me "I want to eat your ass." Oh yikes!!!! That sounds like a great idea. My eyes light up and I enthusiastically nod yes. It's amazing how easily I can lip-read that comment. It's so clear. After lunch, we're walking to the car. I notice an interesting article in a newspaper box. I bend over to read the first couple paragraphs. My husband finds a comfortable bench seat from which he can watch my ass. When I'm done reading, I straighten up and walk over to him seated on the bench. He tells me these were the most memorable three minutes of his life sitting on the bench enjoying looking at my ass. He says, "It's great to be alive." He now knows what people mean when they say that.

We're driving home, and his hand is resting on my thigh.

Him – I like to feel the heat rise from your thigh.

Yes, my thighs are heated right now. I start stroking his dick. I'm gently pinching the tip, and pulling him up through his shaft. Although dickie's bent over to the side, it keeps getting larger, and stronger. He sticks his hand inside his pants, and straightens out dickie. That's better. Now I have more room with which to work. I'm looking forward to a great sex session. It's been some time since our last session, and I'm really looking forward to a great fuck. I'm really ready, and waiting. I'm thinking to myself that first I would like to fuck in the pussy. Before the pussy sex culminates, we can switch dickie to the ass. My pussy and my ass are screaming for dickie's attention. I don't know whose call is stronger, but usually the pussy goes first. I guess that's been the routine so far. I'm fine with either one. But they need to wait till we have privacy. Shit! This waiting is really hard!

We finally have privacy in the house. He bolts the front door, and walks towards the bedroom but stops in the hallway.

Him – I better get our stuff. It'll get messy.

He goes to the bathroom, and gets our basket of lubes and some towels. He says that he wants to take his time. He wants to do this right. He's starved for me. I'm starved for him too. We undress. He pauses to watch me unzip, and pull down my Levi's jeans. He said the day has been a long, slow, torturous burn because he has had to watch my ass walk around in those nice tight Levi's jeans. Levi's are his favorite brand of jeans to admire on my ass. He wants a better backside view of me disrobing, and sits down on the bed to watch. He wants my ass to be at his eye level. He wants to watch me put my jeans back on. He likes to watch me wiggle into my tight jeans, and hop around the room, shaking my ass, all while trying to fit into my tight jeans. That's a vision he loves to keep inside his head. He says it's a pick-me-up to think about this when things get rough at work. I'm glad I can help.

I decide to pull out a clean pair of jeans that might give him the full experience he's looking for. I stand in front of him, with my backside at eye level to his face. I bend over, and pull one pant leg over one foot, and pull it up to my knee. I do the same with the other leg. I grab the waist of the jeans with one have on each side and pull up with both hands while straightening up my body. The jeans glide over my calves, and then slow down on my thighs. That's where the real curves start. The jeans keep catching on my curves, so I need to quick-shimmy in order to loosen the catch. I have lots of curves, so I need to do lots of shimmying, and shaking, in order to pull the jeans up, and over, my hips and ass. Ahhhhhhh. Finally. The jeans are over my hips. I try to bring the top front snaps together, but the jeans need loosening. I bend over again, and stick my butt out. I give it a quick, yet firm, shake. There. That should stretch and loosen the jeans in all the right places. I straighten up again, and pull the front snaps together. It works. The snaps come together. I can suck in my stomach in order to zip up the jeans. I'm good. I'm good.

Surprisingly, and with much effort, these jeans still fit. I didn't have to embarrass myself by not fitting into them. Sometimes I try them on only to realize that my ass is a little bigger than the last time I tried them on. But this time it works. I'm happy. I turn around to look at my husband. He's sitting on the bed, looking at my ass, and his jaw is wide open. He realizes that I'm looking at him, and I'm done putting on my jeans. I twirl around for him to get a 360 degree view. He catches his breath, and tells me to get on the bed, on my back. I start to take off my jeans with the same process I used when I put them on. My husband's still watching my ass. I basically shake off the jeans. The curves that the jeans encountered on the way up, are the same ones the jeans encounter on the way down. I shimmy, and shake, and pull the jeans down. The pants eventually drop down to the floor. I take off my red thong, and fling it onto the floor near the door. I hop into bed. I spread my legs, and wait for him to get in bed with me. He positions his face right in front of my pussy.

Him – Your pussy smells so good. The show will start in a minute after I drink you in.

He kisses my inside thighs, then my pussy. He licks my pussy. Slowly. Up and down. Ahhhhhhhhh. It's been a long time. Side to side. Round and round. He kisses my pussy lips, up and down, slowly. His hands gently grab my hips. My pussy grabs for him.

Him – You taste so good.

His right hand runs up to my breast, and then down to my hip. I feel flutters flying around my pussy. I gently push my pussy towards his mouth, and keep it there. If he needs a better position, then I hope I'm giving it to him.

His tongue goes further into my pussy. He sucks on my lips. My legs go up. His tongue goes up and down, in between my lips. His nose gets in on the stroking for variety. Ohhhhhhhhh!!! This feels so good!!! His tongue wallows around inside my pussy. It wanders wherever it wants to go. Slight sucking here, and there, and I'm in heaven.

Him – I think I'm going to move you to your tummy for a bit.

I turn to lay on my tummy. He sees my ass.

Him – It's too magnificent. I need to take a picture.

Imagine that! He loves the sight of my naked ass so much that he wants to take a picture of it! Maybe all that exercising does pay off. He takes a picture, or two, or three.

Him – You have a big ass. When I say "big", I mean "p-h big", as in p-h phat.

Oh. I'm glad he explained what he meant when he called my ass big. At first I didn't realize that he meant it as a compliment. He puts down his phone, and comes up, over me. His body follows mine. My ass grabs, but it grabs at nothing. Ugh!!!!

Him – Uh oh. I feel that vice getting started.

He tongues my ass. He grabs my ass with his hands. Big butt massage. That's big, as in p-h big.

Him – I'm obsessed with your ass.

He tongues my ass. Holy shit that feels fantastic! That's a harbinger of things to come. His hands run around underneath me to my pussy and start to stroke my clitoris. This is heaven. He reaches towards my head, and grabs a big handful of hair and he pulls back on it. I don't know why I love this, but I do.

Me – Uhhhhhhhhh!! You're making me melt.

He massages my buttocks, while rimming my asshole. I try to grab him with my legs, and surround him.

Me – Oooooooooh…….. This is wonderful….. Aaaaaaaaaaaaah……. Mmmmmmmmmmm….

My ass tries to grab at something, but gets nothing. He mounts my back, and sandwiches my ass between his knees. I feel dickie press against my ass, but he's not inside. Not yet, anyway. My ass tries to grab for him, but, again, nothing. Dickie's getting harder and fills my butt crack. My ass swishes from side to side, trying to catch dickie in the hole. I guess it's a type of reverse basketball game. Get the hoop on the ball, er dick.

My husband sits up, and spreads my cheeks apart with his hands. I feel either dickie or his fingers near my ass. I can't see anything, so all I can do is feel, and imagine. Something's definitely there, and my ass wants it inside of her!!! Quick grabs and pulls. Lots of them. He spreads my cheeks, and I have nothing to grab.

Him – Want to go straight to dickie?

Me – Yes. I do.

Him – Thanks for letting me know. Now I'm going to make you wait. But not for too long. There's only so long that I can wait for you. I can only desire you for so long before I need to have you. You're just that way.

He gets up off the bed, and sorts thru the lube basket. He looks thru the rubbers, and finds a lambskin. That's his favorite. That's my favorite too. He opens the packet.

Me – Let me know where you want me on the bed.

Him – That's fine. Right where you are.

He chooses the Gun Oil as the lube du jour. Good choice! He puts on the rubber, and squirts lube all over the rubber, and my asshole. He says he'll lay on top of me when I'm on my tummy, and let me jack myself off with his dick inside me. That sounds like a great idea. I move the pillow from underneath my face. I need that room to move. He straddles my ass, and rubs his dick around my butthole. Butthole's a little tight. He has to push dickie inside butthole with a little more force than usual. As he does so, I melt. The feeling suddenly overcomes me as dickie enters my asshole. My head falls to the bed, and my arms stretch out. I'm surprised at how relaxed I feel. It's really amazing. Dickie goes in, and out, slowly, and carefully. Just the tip-and-an-inch at first. The relaxing feeling segues into "want". No, it segues into "need". No, it segues into "demand". Yes, I "demand" my ass to pull in dickie. My ass needs to reach into its deepest darkest poo, and engage those muscles. They need to somehow grab dickie, and pull him inside to pound those pleasure points. That's what I want!!! I need to be a ruthless killer shark when chasing my orgasm. I need to go after it with everything I've got. I'm doing it. My ass is grabbing. My inner ass is having a harder time grabbing because the muscles are hard to target. I guess I fumble around a lot, but those muscles are hard to reach. But every time they reach and engage on dickie, then the most intense, but fleeting, feeling overcomes the area of my inside muscles. It's as if I'm trying to pull dickie inside my ass to stroke my clitoris from the inside. But fuck!!! That feels fantastic!!! It's a minor orgasm. If only this feeling lasted longer than a second or two.

All of a sudden, he requests a break. My ass squeezed his balls so hard that he requests a break. Huh? Is he describing "crushed nuts"? We lay next to each other on the bed, and rest for a while. We chat. We snuggle. I find that my leg is rubbing his leg, up and down. He says he has to get back to work – meaning me. Oh – THAT kind of work. My favorite kind of work. I ask for pussy sex. He says first he wants to eat some pussy, and then give me an anal orgasm. He says his balls are still a little sore. My ass is really strong, and squeezed the shit out of his balls.

Me - Dickie was inside of my ass, and the balls are hanging around outside when I'm getting pounded. How did THEY get squeezed? My muscles can't reach outside my ass perimeter.

My husband explained what happened. My butt-cheeks are incredibly powerful. When my asshole clamps down on dickie, then the buttcheeks clench together hard and act like a vice. The buttcheeks slam together and flatten whatever's between them like pancakes with each clench. After repeated vice-like smushing, his balls began to hurt.

Me – Ok. That sounds like a real problem. I'm starting to understand. Maybe it's time for a break.

I'm laying on my back. He puts lube on my pussy, and then licks everything, everywhere. A fingertip rims my ass. It rims everything down there. Then the fingertip slides inside my ass. This is the good stuff.

His tongue circles my clitoris. His finger wiggles its way up my ass, one joint at a time. My legs relax, and widen. They fall further to the sides. My ass starts to pull the finger inside. But the finger disappeared. I don't feel it anymore. The tongue keeps tonguing. There's that finger again. He sucks on my clitoris with his tongue. His other hand wanders around, and inside, my pussy. Holy shit!!! The two-hole feeling is wonderful! Two-holing isn't twice the pleasure, it's a hundred times the pleasure. And this activity doesn't even involve dickie. Not yet anyway. He starts to focus on my pussy, on my G spot. Oooooooohhh!!! He's pushing on that knob. He primed the knob, and now it squirts its juices with every push on it. I feel the juices collect inside of me. If I'm feeling that, then there must be lots of juices, and they're flowing all over.

I stop him, and tell him I want pussy sex. He says his balls are still tender from my ass vice grabbing him earlier. I feel his balls with my fingertips. Yes, they are tender. My ass did all that damage? As my favorite bad-boy entertainer Shaggy sings, and I say the same thing, "It wasn't me." I'm amazed at all the issues that surface when we're having great sex. I tell him that he needs to blow his load in order to feel better. I use both hands to get dickie nice and hard and ready for pussy. As soon as dickie's ready, he tells me to lay on my back. That would be easiest right now. I do exactly that.

Dickie enters pussy, and I'm feeling fantastic. I live for this!!! I hope it feels as good for him, as it does for me. He pumps away, and I can feel him getting bigger with each pump. I look into his eyes and smile. I'm a happy woman. He finally blows, and the pumping slows down. I stretch my arms above my head and relax. I'm a happy woman, and he's a happy man.

4 STRONG FEELINGS

He's been staring at my ass all day long. Ok, I admit it. I deliberately put on my extra tight yoga pants strictly for his viewing pleasure. I like for him to enjoy me. I want him to enjoy me. He's my husband, he's supposed to enjoy me. He says the sight of my ass disturbs him to an irreparable degree. Sometimes he's had enough. That's a good thing. I like that. That's when things get interesting.

I'm sleeping in my bed, under the hot, tall covers. I've been sleeping for a while, so the bed and the comforter are fully and thoroughly heated. I like to sleep when I'm hot under the covers. It's nothing sexual. I just like the heat. It allows me to enjoy a deep sleep. Someone's moving my covers around. Must be the dog. He must be walking around the room looking for a place to lay down. I wish he wouldn't jar me out of my wonderful sleep. I instantly go back to sleep. Someone's moving my covers around. Oh, it's my husband. It's nice that he's here, but I wish I weren't jarred out of my sleep. I go back to sleep. The bed is losing heat. I stir. Oh, that's my husband again. He's kneeling next to the bed, and his hands are reaching under my covers. He's searching for something. Oh! He's searching for me!! He finds my right thigh, and, with his fingertips, gives it a soft, firm rub - a finder's rub. The room is dark, and I can't see anything, but I'm guessing by his touch that he likes what he's found. His other hand finds the small of my back, and, with the flat of his hand, gives it a firm finder's rub. I drift back to sleep. I don't know why I drift back to sleep. This really isn't a good time to go back to sleep, but I do. I can't help myself. Eventually I drift back awake. His fingers find my legs, and feel around, up and down my thighs. He quietly pushes the covers off me, but just enough for him to explore. He knows how much I love the hot covers, and tries to economize the heat for me. He climbs onto the bed from the end and kneels at my feet. He unfolds my legs, and spreads them. He puts his nose right between my legs and deeply inhales.

Him - Ahhhh! That's it! That's my wife!

He sits up and lightly massages my legs, up and down.

Him – Let's pull these pants off. I want to get inside of them.

He grabs the bottom of each pant leg and pulls. I lift my ass, and pull off my thong, along with the pants. He won't be getting a good look at that. Well, not this time anyway. The pants are thrown on the floor. He gently pushes my knees apart, and bends down to be in between my thighs. He inhales again. His tongue wanders around, searching for my clitoris. His hands lightly massage the insides of my thighs. His hands wander to my ass area. He's using lots of things to search for lots of things all at the same time. I'm glad he's so creative. His fingers glide over my asshole. The tops of his fingers, then the flip side of his fingers. Now that he's found my clitoris, he tongues it, this time with a gentle sucking action. His fingers swipe my pussy lips, up and down. Then they swipe the insides of the pussy lips, and glide up and down.

He puts a lubeless finger inside of my ass. It's dry, so he says he needs to get some lube. I agree. As he gets up, he insists to turn on the light. I tell him no. He says he wants to see what he's doing. I relent. I'm enjoying myself too much to protest. He comes back in the room with our fun box. There's a nice selection of lubes and condoms in there. He pulls out a water-based lube – the good stuff. The party stuff. He settles himself back on the bed, in between my legs, right where he wants to be. He lays on his tummy, and his face is planted in front of my pussy. He runs his hands up and down my outer thighs, and then up and down my inner thighs. That feels fantastic!! He squirts some lube on my asshole, and then on his fingertip. His fingers find my asshole. He swirls his finger around the outside of my asshole, to cover both with lube - his finger and my asshole. He slides one finger inside my asshole, but only an inch deep. I'm sure it's one finger, but it might be more. Sometimes I'm wrong. But it sure feels right.

He accidentally gets lube on the clit, and decides to switch from his tongue to his finger. One finger swiping my clit. One finger up my ass. He very slowly swipes my clitoris, and very gradually increases the rate. The swipes are segueing into a frenzy. My insides are going crazy! He starts to vigorously masturbate my clitoris with his finger. At least he's using something that works. My asshole involuntarily pulls on his finger, but his finger stays put. Shucks! I try again with the same result. My ass muscles try a slightly different angle. There's the pull. But his finger stays put. Shucks!! Now I'm getting agitated. I pull with all of my ass muscles, the outer ones, and the deep inner ones. He's particularly stingy with his finger. Now I'm going all out to pull his finger inside my asshole. My asshole and my Gluteus Maximus muscles tighten. His fingers don't budge. My mind is going berserk! I can do this! I know I can! My asshole and Gluteus Maximus and leg muscles tighten. He keeps stroking my clitoris. Those amazing feelings are wafting throughout my insides. I know I can get many more feelings if only I go all in, with everything, and anything. My legs tighten and straighten. It's just easier that way. I need to get a better grip on his finger. I try again. I tighten every muscle I have inside of me, and outside of me, and my ass. I tighten my leg muscles. I tighten my all-body muscles. I tighten every muscle that I have!! Pull!!!

There's a strong taste of THAT feeling. It's a small orgasm. I taste it inside of my asshole. That's where it's starting. It's a slight rumble, much like the small shockwaves that come right before a major earthquake. But these waves aren't a warning sign. They're a sign of good things to come. The cliff is near. I peek over the cliff. One more pull, and I'm over that cliff. I go all-in with every muscle that I have. I clench my ass, my legs, my arms, my fists, my brain. My asshole pulls on his finger, and I fall over the cliff. Oh my God!!! It's the "Holy Shit!!!" moment!!! I'm cumming like a ton of bricks. Those soaring feelings glide around my private area, and pulsate extreme pleasure throughout my body and my brain, and every existential part of me. My private area feels as if it's the inside of a washing machine filled with hot water, and bubbly, slippery soap, being turned over and over, around and around, every which way only it's hot pleasure and relaxation rather than water and soap. They soak thru everything, again and again, thoroughly mulching and swishing and mixing everything together. The energy is just as forceful and random and scrambled together as the clothes are, when they loop around, and wind about, in the washing machine. I become a pleasurable mush. It's absolutely amazing! I'm yelling and screaming. I can't help it. It feels soooooooooo good!!!! My throat hurts from all of the screaming, but I keep screaming. Those feelings are so fantastic that they force me to scream. Oh, to live like this, every minute of every day.

He could feel how frustrated my ass was, but he knew he had to stick with it. My ass was wide open, and was more ready for dickie, than a finger. My ass was so open and relaxed that it could barely catch his one finger, much less squeeze it. However, he was going to be stingy with his finger, and finish me off this way.

The feelings start to fade. Yikes! What can I do to extend them!!!! Do I pull on my ass muscles?? Which ones? All of them? My ass muscles are way too relaxed to do anything. They won't budge for anything right now. They're mushy mush mush, and I guess so am I. Maybe I'll just enjoy the trip. That was definitely an orgasm. I know my asshole's wide open. I don't have to ask. I know. I relax. I slump to my side. But why was I yelling?!? I groaned. I yelled. I yelled at the top of my lungs. My yelling even startled ME. I really need to shut up because the neighbors might hear. And if they hear me yell, then they'll know what we're doing. At least I hope they'll know what we're doing, and not think it's a domestic violence issue. I don't know which is worse. But I know that I couldn't stop yelling. And I was LOUD!! This feeling was way too wonderful to be quiet about it. Well, I'll worry about that later. Now I'm just going to enjoy myself. I have nothing left in me. I'm all fucked out. I can't move, but I have to know,

Me – How was that for you?

Him – What?

Me – I was going thru a lot back there. I was wondering, how it was for you? What did you see?

Him – I'm just doing my job.

He's fingering my asshole. He says he still wants to play with my ass a bit. The hole's relaxed, and he wants to play. Once I have an anal orgasm, then the hole goes back to normal size pretty quickly. Either my husband has to move fast, or there's no room for dickie anymore. Sometimes it's very clear I've had enough. Right now is one of those times. I drift into my happy place to enjoy the pleasures I was just given. It's clear to me that I have the best husband ever!

I clean up, and put on a fresh pair of pajamas. I can move now, but I'm still all fucked out. That's clear. I'm pretty sure my eyes are still crossed because it's hard to see out of them. I'll just keep my eyes closed. I'm so glad that the only place I have to go is the bed. I don't want to meet people, and have to tone down these fabulous feelings.

Me – That was the orgasm to end all orgasms.

Him – We'll do that again. It's nice to make my wife cum after twenty five years together.

Me – That was so fucking amazing.

Once you experience one of these orgasms, you don't need anything else. Of course other types of orgasms offer different feelings. They're fantastic in their own right. But this orgasm is the top of the top. It's a super elaborate supreme Orgasm. The best of the best. Now I'm finding myself disturbed to an irreparable degree. I guess you can call that karma. I've just had the best of the best of orgasms, and now I'm the one that's wonderfully disturbed.

There's no going back to mediocre orgasms. I'm going to have to have this type of orgasm again. That's why I wrote down this episode – so I can brief myself before we try again, and to let my husband know what I experienced. After all, he wants to know. I love my husband. He's the best!!

5 FULL BUSH

He comes into the bedroom wearing his pajamas and a bathrobe over them. He never wears a bathrobe over his pajamas. I wonder why he's doing so now. It's sort of a Hugh Hefner look. I like it. I stand and face him. I wasn't doing anything important anyway – putting away clothes. He places his arms around my waist and kisses my lips. He whispers to me that I look hot in my yoga pants, and my ass is the best ass he's ever seen.

He tells me he wants to rub one out for me.

Me – Oh?! Wow!!

He pulls down my yoga pants to my thighs.

Him – You're going commando?!?

Me – Ummmmmm…..yes.

His hand rubs my pussy. His other hand stays around my waist.

Him – How many hairs do you have down here?

Me – A full bush.

Him – That's the way I like it!

His fingers find my clitoris and start to rub it, up and down. His other hand grabs my ass. I turn to my side to make it easier for him to reach around. His fingers slide down to my asshole. One finger slides just a short distance inside. I think I know where he's going with this. It feels fantastic!

I reach into his pants and find his hard cock. He's not going commando. He's wearing underwear. I grab his cock, and I start rubbing it up and down. With my other hand, I grab his balls, and give both of them a gentle squeeze, over and over again.

He says we need lube. He goes into the bathroom to get our lube basket.

We both squirt some lube onto each of our hands, and get back to the action. He's moaning and groaning. His dick's getting really hard. He tells me he's going to cum soon. I tell him that's the point. He says it'll be messy. I tell him we'll clean it up.

He tells me to sit on the bed, and leads me there. I spread my bathrobe on the bed and sit down. He gently pushes me to lay down, and finds my clit again with his fingers. He starts his special rubbing. His other fingers find my asshole. He's fingering that too. Oh! THIS is what he came to do. He really is here to rub one out for me! Yahoo!! We don't have much time so I'm concerned whether or not I will orgasm.

I start to clench my insides. I realize that I need to straighten my legs, but they're hanging off the side of the bed. I straighten them, and soon realize that they need to lay on something. It's hard for me to strain, and clench my legs at the same time. I tell my husband I need to rotate, and fully lay on the bed. He agrees, and helps me do so. He repositions himself and his hands and fingers. I pull the pillow out from under my head because I realize I need to be absolutely straight to clench everything. For some reason I was made that way.

He had just given me the exact same orgasm a couple days ago. It's hard to say that this is the same orgasm as before, because no two orgasms are exactly alike. That's the core of nature. But the approach is certainly the same, or very similar. I remember exactly how to clench my body, and pull on my asshole. I'm repeating what I did the previous time. It's working. The feelings are starting to come back with every clench. They're building, and building on top of each other. I'm pulling the penultimate pull. One more pull and I'm over that cliff. Here it comes ……. Aaaaaaaaaaaaaaaaaahhhhhhhhhhhhh!! I'm over that cliff! Pleasure and relaxation waft thru my private areas. I toss and I turn. I'm holding in a scream. I wonder why I'm not screaming out loud. Oh!! Those fantastic feelings!

I'm recovering. I look at the time. Wow!!! He rubbed

one out for me in less than fifteen minutes!! That's absolutely unbelievable!! I tell him so. He says we don't have lots of time, but he wanted to do that for me. I'm a lucky woman! He says he usually likes to take lots more time to let the feelings build and build. It seems that the more time is spent on building the feelings, the bigger the orgasm I experience. Oh, so that's how it works. The time and effort put into the initial building of feelings is directly proportional to the strength of the orgasm. That makes sense.

But, oh!! The possibilities! If my husband can get me to orgasm in about fifteen minutes time, then I am the luckiest woman in the world!! I have the best husband in the whole wide world!

Both my ass, and I, feel fantastic for days afterward. I'm so satiated, for so long, that it's really amazing. My sexual needs are addressed, and not repressed. What a concept! It seems as if all of the time and effort put into all of the previous sessions really paid off. At first, we were simply noodling around. The more noodling around we did, then we gradually picked up more and more techniques. Eventually we come to this – The Russian Feather Orgasm in about fifteen minutes. Now that's amazing!!

6 CHOCOLATE ANNIVERSARY

We're driving home after a full day of friends and museums. We're looking forward to celebrating our one year chocolate anniversary of having anal sex by having anal sex. That's appropriate and expected.

Him – I want to taste your pussy and your ass tonight.

I think about what he just said. I'm sure I can help him with that. As I'm driving the car, I hold my left hand on the steering wheel, and with my right hand, I reach down into my pants. My fingers find my pussy lips and spread them, gently rub between them, gathering pussy juice on them. I gather my wet fingers inside the cup of my hand and pull my hand out of my pants. I reach for my husband's nose and gently wipe my wet finger underneath his nose. He grabs my hand, and sucks on my fingers with his lips. He says he wants more.

Him – Where did you learn that?

Me – I just thought of it.

When we get home, I go to the bathroom to rinse my backside. I can't see back there, so I just wash it. It's easiest that way. He comes into the bathroom.

Him – Let's take our clothes off.

Me – Ok. Do I leave my bra on?

Him – Yes. Those girls bounce around a lot. They need to be contained.

We take off our own clothes, and each other's clothes, and throw them on the ground. We turn to each other. I grab his dick, stroke his dick, finger his tip, and gently squeeze his balls. He turns me away from him and grabs my ass. I lean over the counter, and his fingers enter my pussy. He fingers my G spot, and gets my insides feeling good. I'm moaning, and groaning. I feel the juices pool inside of me. They overflow. I feel the juices run down my leg. I feel them squirt out of me. Wow! I never felt that before. I feel like I'm peeing. But I'm not peeing. And it feels so much better than peeing. But the good feeling is stronger than the running down my leg feeling. I keep going.

My natural lubes are in full force, and all over me, and over the floor. I'd better watch my step, or else I can slip. He keeps fingering my pussy and I keep squirting all over. This is insane! I guess the more he fingers me, the more I squirt. It was just a couple months ago that he tried this new technique, and I simply became wet. Now I squirt all over the floor. That's a big difference. That's big progress.

He takes me to the bedroom. I already have the sheets prepared, and the blanket put down.

Him – Where do you want to start?

Me – I want to get fucked in my pussy, and then fucked in my butt. That's what I want to do.

Him – Ok, but first I want to taste your ass and your pussy.

He positions his face in between my legs and starts tonguing my clitoris. Oh, the good feelings are starting again. He tongues my asshole too. Uhhhhhhhhhh! Ha! That feels fantastic. I make every effort to enjoy these feelings to the fullest. He tongues my clitoris again, and inserts his thumb in my ass. My ass situates his thumb inside of me. I can feel the good feelings start to gather. I need to pull with my inside asshole muscles. I pull. Nothing. I pull. Not much. I keep pulling. I realize I need to straighten my legs. I straighten my right leg. My husband rotates his body, and slides off the bed without stopping what he's doing. I grab his dick, and start stroking it. I know he likes gentle stroking so I try to do the gentle stroking. But my mind is feverish, and I hope I'm not getting too rough for him.

Me – That's enough. I want pussy sex.

For some reason, I can't talk, so I use my forefingers from each hand to point towards my pussy. My request should be very obvious. He smiles and nods yes.

Him – You want my dick in your pussy?

I enthusiastically nod yes. I spread my legs to receive him. He comes between them, and positions dickie in my pussy. Dickie's nice and hard. Our sex life has been on a holiday schedule due to the holidays. I didn't like that at all. That means we were "enjoying the holidays" instead of having sex. But anyway, dickie feels absolutely fantastic inside my pussy! At first, my husband pumps slowly, and eventually gets faster, and faster. I love to fuck, and I know it! My husband knows it too. Dickie pops out.

Him – Do you want to try doggie style?

Me – Sure.

I get off the bed, and bend over the side. I stick my ass in the air, trying to get the right height for dickie to enter. My husband wastes no time in finding my pussy with his dick, and puts it right inside. He starts to pump away. I bury my face in the mattress. I love to fuck. He grabs my hips, and keeps pumping faster, and faster. I try to keep rhythm with his movements. He's pounding me. The feelings feel so fantastic that I find myself screaming. Screaming with ecstasy. He says he's going to blow soon. I tell him to go ahead. His dick is so big inside of me, that it feels like a big piston pumping away. He's hitting all of my pussy pleasure points all at the same time. I'm screaming at the tops of my lungs. The pumping is slowing down. His dick is feeling looser inside of me. Eventually we both fall onto the bed, together, next to each other. We rest. We need to. We have no other option.

Me – So you used the Gun Oil?

Him – No, I didn't use any lube.

Me – What?!? I get juicy, but I need lube, and lots of it. It felt so good, I didn't realize you did that.

We lay next to each other, I'm on my right side. My arms extend over his chest.

Him – What was your favorite part?

Me – The fucking, and the pounding. What was your favorite part?

Him – Tasting pussy and ass.

Him – We need to get ready to go out to dinner, and celebrate our one year chocolate anniversary.

Me – But we didn't have anal sex on our one year chocolate anniversary… We can have anal sex, and maybe only anal sex… no pussy sex…. during our next session. We're no longer on holiday hours, so it will be in a couple days.

Him – Ok.

7 SUSHI AND SEX

My husband and I are at a restaurant enjoying a private dinner. It's just the two of us, and it's a completely unexpected sushi dinner, with a Chekov play afterwards. The play was planned, the sushi wasn't. I love sushi. My favorite date is "Sex and Sushi", but it seems the sex might be scheduled for a separate evening. Since we're already having sushi, that means we skipped the "sex" part. We can't even invert that sequence, because we're going out to a play afterwards. That's disappointing, but not all is lost. The dinner's very romantic, with heavily dimmed lighting, white tablecloths, and lots of dishes. This restaurant was his idea, and I can't help but wonder if he wants to get inside my pants. I'm wondering if all I have is sex on my mind. We've had an extended dry spell because of the holidays. We were on a holiday schedule, which drastically interfered with our sex life. When in public, I should keep those thoughts to myself, but I'm with my husband so I can speak up, quietly. Well, he's my husband and I'm looking forward to the possibility of sex tonight. He knows he can have sex with me anytime he wants it, but he still goes way out of his way to romance me, and dine me, and treat me like a lady, the love of his life. I'm a very lucky woman, and I feel lucky that we're going out for a sushi dinner, because that's my favorite food. I excuse myself to go to the bathroom, and I get a text when I'm in the washroom.

6:34 pm text from him – I want to suck your pussy and tongue fuck your fondue pot.

Holy shit!!! That's absolutely unexpected!! Wow!! But I'm thinking of the possibilities!! If he's thinking it, and texting it, then he must want to do it. That's clear!! Now I know he's trying to get inside my pants! Before, I wasn't sure, but now I am. Huuuuuuuuuuuuh! I'm a very lucky woman! I LOVE IT!!!

I text him back – It's a date!!!!

I go back to the table. Our conversation has taken on a different atmosphere. We talk all sorts of sex talk. The couple at the table next to us is discussing their "don", which I realized is short for "sperm donor." I'd much rather be having our conversation. I'm a little sad that we didn't have chocolate sex during our chocolate sex anniversary. He agrees. He said we celebrate the anniversary of our wedding, our first kiss, and our first chocolate sex. He decides that we need to have more anniversaries to celebrate. He'll think about what else we should celebrate. I love to celebrate with him, so I steadfastly agree. Prolonged sex talk is a great way to get both of us fired up, even if we're not planning on acting on any of it. Any length of interesting sex talk will do that, and our conversations are very interesting. We finish dinner. We attend a play that wasn't very good. We thought about leaving during the intermission, but decided to stay for the end. It was ok. We go home. Both of us are exhausted, and too tired, to do anything. That really sucks, but sometimes that's the case. He won't be going to sleep because he has a big work project he has to finish by the morning. So I go to sleep, and he gets to working.

10:17 pm text from him – I have a taste for your big beautiful luscious ass. I want to lick it up and down and then slide my tongue inside it and fuck it till you come.

OMG!!! That's a steamy text!!! That's reminiscent of a raunchy blues song, Candylicker. I love Blues music!! I love sex!! There's lots of sex in the Blues. Unfortunately, I don't even know I received that text, because I'm sleeping comfortably in my bed. He comes into my bedroom, and searches for me under the covers. I stir. I realize he's there, searching for me. Did he finally come to his senses, and want to fuck?

Him – I sent you a text.

Me – I didn't get it.

Him – Read it.

I grab my phone and read the text on the cover. Wow!!!! He tells me he wants to rub one out for me. I tell him I want to fuck. Next thing I know is I'm laying on our bed, on my back. He's licking my clitoris, and has two fingers up my ass. I'm reaching, and I'm cumming. It's not the explosive orgasm, but it's a strong one. Surprisingly, because it's not a super orgasm, it can be enjoyed over a much longer period of time. I'm grabbing with my pussy, and then with my ass. I straighten my legs. But that doesn't help much. Without stopping his work in progress, he gets up off the bed, and twirls his body to be perpendicular to mine. With my hand, I grab dickie, and the balls. I use my fingertips to gently massage dickie's head. I cup the balls in my hand. I pump his shaft. I can feel him harden. He's super hard. He's the good-fucking kind of hard.

Me – I want pussy sex.

Him – It's not a good time of the month. You might get pregnant.

Me – Then I want butt sex. I bought the economy-sized box of rubbers. We have lots of them - lambskin, the ultra thin kind, and whatever else is in there. There should be lots of feeling. That'll be fine.

He has two fingers up my ass, up to their knuckles, palm up. It feels so fantastic! He keeps rubbing something inside of me. I keep pulling with my ass muscles. This is the technique to get me to explode with orgasm. I want that orgasm. This is my opportunity. I ask if my ass is open, and he tells me yes. But I can still grab with my ass, and get some feeling out of my efforts. I get small bursts of that orgasm, but the full orgasm doesn't come. Believe it or not, it's ok, because I'm enjoying myself immensely. My eyes roll around inside my head. My neck pushes my head back. My back arches. My legs are wide open, and welcoming. My insides are at full-intensity feeling. It fills my entire private area with absolute full pleasure. It sticks around instead of dissipating. The feelings aren't hyper strong, but they're strong nonetheless. The feelings are plenty strong, and they last, and they last, and they last. They keep going, and going, and going. I want to live my life feeling this way. The orgasm trade-off is duration versus intensity. That's a good trade-off, because it adds lots of unexpected variety to our sex life. My husband's really good at sex, but even he can't predict what kind of orgasm he'll give me, or even if he gives me one at all. There are way too many unknowns at play. All we can do is try, and practice, and enjoy ourselves. That's a big part of the fun of our sex life. We are never sure of what's going to happen, but we keep trying. There are surprises at every session, no matter how experienced we are. The feelings begin to subside.

He keeps his fingers inside my ass, and uses his other fingers to massage my G-spot, which is way up my pussy. I don't know how he does it, but he's stroking my clitoris too. I'm thinking that all his years of guitar playing really help our sex life.

I grab dickie with my hand, and pump him until he cums. I can feel the wetness thru his underwear, and thru his fleece pajamas. I'm glad he came. Many times he holds it in, and that's not right. He should feel good, just like I do. I've had enough, and so has he. I slump to my side. I'm all fucked out. When he gets my G-spot to squirt out all of its contents, then I'm easily all fucked out. That tends to satisfy me for days afterwards. It completely exhausts me, and I'm a happy woman. When people see me, they like me, but they don't know what they like about me. Unless, of course, they know what all-fucked-out looks like. They somehow know how to read my facial expressions and body language. But not many people are at the same level we're at. He gets up and goes to the bathroom to clean up. Slowly I stir, and start to get my senses back.

Me – You came even though dickie wasn't super hard. I didn't know that could happen.

Him – He only gets super hard when he's having fun inside pussy or butt.

Me – Oh. You massaged my G-spot. Did I squirt all over?

Him – Why? Are the sheets wet?

Me – I haven't checked yet.

Him – Yeah, you squirted right into my hand.

After a pause, he comments thoughtfully – My wife loves to fuck.

Him – You need to delete those texts in case the kids look at your phone.

I guess there's lots and lots of cleanup after one of our sex sessions. He watches me delete the texts, but I first copy them into my writing folder to access later when I have more time. That's really good material, and I'll want to write about this session in the morning. He gets back to work, and I go back to sleep. A deep, deep, luxurious sleep.

8 THE KICKSTARTER

I have a coffee date with a friend at 1pm. Afterwards I need to pick up my kids from school at 3pm. Then it's numerous after-school activities, at-home dinner, and homework, the usual. I have a very busy schedule today.

My husband calls me from work around 11am. He tells me he needs to see me and that's why he's coming home from work early. Can I please pick him up from the train at noon? Whoa!! That's a real come-on! I give him a firm "Yes! I'm looking forward to it!!" I look thru my underwear drawer, and find the black and red thong with the big black bow on the back. My husband gave me that thong as a special sexy gift. He said he wanted to wrap my ass in ribbons. That's the thong that today's surprise occasion calls for. I put it on. It's the right occasion for it. I have a feeling this session will kickstart our sex life back into high gear after having suffered thru an extended holiday season hiatus.

I text my friend to cancel our coffee date. I told her something came up. I didn't tell her what. She's an adult. She can figure out this stuff. No need to ask for specifics.

I pick up my husband from the train, and tell him I'm super glad he came home early. We head home. The kids are in school, meaning out of the house, so we have given ourselves the ultimate gift of luxury – sex without any interruptions. Yay!!!!

We go into the bedroom. Both of us are very excited at our luck. I grab him around the shoulders. I bear hug him. I'm super excited. It's January, and for the entire month of December, we had to abide by our Holiday Schedule when it came to sex, meaning, we didn't have any. There were way too many activities, and not enough time for each other. We're all exhausted. Now both of us are starving for sex. We're feverish with desire.

Him – Where do we start?

Me – I don't know.

Him – I want to lick your ass, and tongue-fuck you.

Me – I want to fuck first in my pussy, and then in my ass.

We can accommodate each and all of our desires. Now that we expressed our expectations, we undress ourselves. Undressing each other is way too much foreplay for this situation. Both of us are too hungry. He admires my thong, and tells me to keep it on. I see the hunger in his eyes.

Me – You want to fuck me with my thong on.

Him – Yes, I love that thong.

I was right to put on that thong. He lays me down on the bed, on my stomach. He bends down to have his face even with my ass. He slides my thong over an inch or two to the left side so his face can gain access to the good stuff. He rims my asshole with his tongue, and then sticks his tongue deep inside my asshole. He goes in and out, in and out, in and out. Yes, I remember this feeling. It's been a long time since I've felt it. It makes me melt!!! He pulls out his tongue, and tells me to flip over onto my back.

I spread my legs to receive him. He says he needs to get some lube. He comes back with our "lube bag". He opens it up, and pulls out the Gun Oil, and some rubbers. The Gun Oil is a clue that my husband means business. I'm glad to see that because so do I. He puts the bottle on the bed near my feet. He climbs onto the bed, and kneels right in between my legs. Now that he's well-situated, he finds my clitoris with his tongue, and sucks away. Uhhhhhhhhh!!!! I'm in ecstasy. It's been way too long!!! I'm overexcited and overeager because I know this session will end our long dry spell. Since we have a couple hours to ourselves, we'll get all of this out of our system.

His fingers take over stroking my clitoris as his tongue wanders from my clitoris to my asshole. He rims my asshole, and pokes his tongue inside again and again. The feelings are gathering. I'm going to go crazy!!! He inserts his fingers into my pussy, and finds my g-spot, hidden all the way up there. When he starts working over my g-spot, I know it will probably end in me squirting all over the place from my Skein's Gland. The Skein's Gland is a bulbous, slimy, hanging ball just below the clitoris. It has a hole for squirting juices. His fingers gently start to pump the hell out of my g-spot. Whenever I feel a rush of relaxation and pleasure, then I know the g-spot is being properly worked, and I'm squirting. I can feel the squirting as a warm sensation inside my pussy. The liquid floods my pussy. This is a fantastic way to get back into the sexy swing of things. My insides will be properly primed when the Skeins Gland is unloaded. The juices that build up in my pussy provide good lube for sex.

It's time to fuck. We both know it.

Him – How do you want to fuck first?

Me – How about doggie style? In the pussy?

Him – Great! Let's do it.

I lean over the bed, ready for him. He loads on the lube, positions himself, and then dickie. Dickie knows where to go. He easily slides right inside pussy. We pump away. We're so sex-starved that we don't even start out slow. We immediately go to medium intensity, and build from there. Lots of lube helps.

Dickie gets big and hard really, really fast. He feels sooooooo good inside of me!! I can't stop. If I'm feeling that way, then I'm sure he's feeling that way too. It's been too long. Dickie's getting really big.

Him – Do you want to switch to the butt?

Hmmmmmmmmmmmmm. I like this thinking. The pussy sex is fantastic, but it's been so long since we've had butt sex. I agree.

Me – Yes. Just switch holes.

There's no reason to switch positions. We're too worked up. Dickie tries to come on in. Butthole is too tight and unrelenting at first. He pinches his tip to get dickie inside of me. No success. He pinches a little more. Finally. Just a little bit of dickie goes inside my asshole. I'm feeling surprisingly full. We let too much time lapse between our butt sessions. He goes in slowly, and after a while slowly starts pumping. The old feelings are starting to build up again. They're surprisingly fleeting and faint. I'm glad we're having butt sex now because if we let too much more time lapse, then I'm not sure what kind of sex shape my ass would be in. My asshole needs a much tighter maintenance sex schedule, otherwise it somehow falls out of its sex-ready shape. When we have a regular schedule, then dickie slips in and out very easily. It's a straight shot in and out, and butt is ready for him at a moment's notice. When too much time passes, then the inside folds and crevices must get out of alignment somehow, and the feeling of fullness fights its way into our session. I prefer to be in tip-top sex shape. I want to get back to the sexy in-and-out feeling. Well, we just need to ass fuck more often from now on. It's that easy.

He's pounding my ass, and looking at my ass at the same time. He's telling me that it's the most beautiful ass he's ever seen in his life. It's HIS ass, and no one else's. He also likes to see fresh sex bruise marks on my hips and ass, because that means we're getting back into a good sex schedule.

He grabs hold of my ass and slams his dick into me. He pumps, and he pumps. I'm trying to catch his rhythm, and make it mine. I succeed more times than not. There's a real hunger in his actions, and that can complicate matters. Dickie's getting super full. He's pounding all of the right pleasure points. And by "all", I mean ALL the right pleasure points. None go unnoticed. I'm screaming from pleasure. I remember this part! I'm so glad he's back in there again! He tells me he's going to blow soon. I feel that he's really big, but I'm glad he's telling me too. He blows, and the rhythm gets slower. Both of us wilt soon afterward.

I fall over onto the bed. I'm all fucked out. He staggers around the room. I tell him to come lay on the bed next to me. I pound a spot on the bed for him with the palm of my hand. He joins me. We cuddle.

Me – That was so amazing!! I'm so glad we're doing this again.

I can see that he's completely spent and tired. He

needs to catch his breath. He lays down next to me. He looks at me and smiles.

Him – My wife's not a plain Jane. She's wired a little differently. A non-union electrician wired her brain. A non-union plumber layed out her pipes.

We rest and laugh and joke around. He starts to play with my pussy, which is still inside my panties. I'm still wearing my thong, unbelievably. It hasn't yet come off. He finds my clitoris, and starts to stroke it again. He's getting me excited again. I'm sure I have more energy left in me, but I'm not as sure about him. He continues playing. Maybe he has more energy than I thought he did.

Him – Your thong's coming off.

He gets up, and pulls off my thong. I raise my ass to help him. He throws my thong onto the ground, anywhere. He gets up off the bed, and walks around to the foot of the bed. He spreads my legs, and goes down on me again with his mouth. My private area feels sparklier, and bubblier, and much more responsive, than the first round we had just a short time ago. It must still be energized from the fuck session we just had. It's all building on each other. There's a lot to build on. A lot is getting built. He puts lots of lube on his fingers. No sex for a long period of time means lots of stuff goes up my ass.

He's tongue-playing my clitoris, and slips a finger up my ass, up to the first knuckle. I grab that finger with all of my mighty ass. That lone finger didn't do much for me, so he took it out, and slipped in his thumb. I grab that thumb. I get slight pleasure. I grab again, and pull with my deep inner muscles. Somehow I need to have something to grab a hold of with my ass, but this something can't go in too deep. My ass needs to work itself into a frenzy, and then the orgasm comes. I ask him to put two fingers inside my ass, and to suck on my clitoris. He obliges. He's so sweet to do this for me. I really appreciate it. I can't get this feeling any other way. I grab with my entire ass. It feels so good, and I feel tingles of an orgasm coming thru.

I ask for a third finger. He gives me a "Flat O". A "Flat O," which we also called "Duckie," is the hand position where all of the tips, of all of the fingers, of one hand, meet all at once and it looks like a duck's beak. He knows what to do to me. After long dry spells, he sometimes gives me a Flat O, which sometimes ends up as a fist. First he'll start with the Flat O, and see where that goes. If I need the fist, then he's prepared to provide that too, but later. He gives me the five finger Flat O right up to the main knuckle. He shimmies it around inside my ass. I grab it with all my might. I keep grabbing. Waves of pleasure float around my ass after each release. This makes for a lovely pattern. I could spend the entire day feeling like this. Lots of pleasure, little bursts of pleasure, then lots of pleasure. There's more room for more fingers because butt's not yet satisfied. He knows what ass likes when she has his fingers inside of her because the inner ass ring becomes thick and strong when it's aroused. But there comes a moment where I must have had enough. I can't believe it, but I ask him to stop. I could go on forever and ever, but I don't want to overindulge at his expense. His neck might hurt tomorrow, and his lips might be chapped. That's too much. But it's hard to know right now what condition he'll be in tomorrow.

Me – Is butt wide open?

Him – She's been open for some time.

Me – Any chance we could have pussy sex again? Is dickie ready? Can he get ready again so soon?

Him – Well, he can get ready….

I know what that means. I jump off the bed, and put lots of lube on both of my hands. I stand in front of my husband, grab dickie with both hands, and start kissing my husband on the neck. I massage and pump dickie with both hands. Up and down. I catch the balls, and gently cup them in one hand, while pumping dickie with my other hand. I gently tug on the tip. The lube feels fantastic. I can feel dickie growing in size and hardness. He's almost ready. Just a little more stroking. He puts his hands on my hands, and gently takes them off dickie.

Him – Ok. He's ready now.

Me – Missionary style?

He smiles and nods. I get back on the bed, sitting on my butt. I spread my legs and arms. I smile at him. I'm eager. He positions himself in between my legs, aligning dickie with pussy, and has them touch. I grab his shoulders with each hand and, gently but firmly, pull him down on me. I lay back too. Dickie easily slides into pussy. I'm loving this!!! I've waited for so long!!! My husband starts pumping, slowly, but gets faster very fast. I try to match his rhythm.

Dickie gets harder and firmer as the rhythm gets faster and faster. I remove the pillow from behind my head. My knees are close to my chest, but I keep my pelvis flat on the bed. I push my butt into the bed. That angle feels absolutely fantastic when dickie is super hard. Dickie pumps and rubs the top length of my vagina, all the way from his tip to his shaft, up and down, up and down, length after length. It's something about dickie's tip, and his inherent lumps and bumps, rolling and bumping, along the tops of pussy's walls, that feels fantastic. Dickie's naturally curved upwards so this applies the right amount of pressure on the pussy roof. The pleasures build on each other, and increase as the pumping continues. Dickie's super hard, and that tells me my husband is enjoying himself. I hear him groaning the most pleasurable groans. I spread my legs open, and as wide, and as flat, as possible. This gives dickie the right angle to rub my pussy walls the best way. My eyes are rolling into the back of my head. My neck is tilting my head back. I'm screaming with pleasure. Dickie keeps going and going. He's hitting those fantastic pleasure streaks up and down the top of my pussy canal!!! Uhhhhhhhhh!!!! He keeps going and going and going… I grab dickie with my pussy. I try to pump that way. This is fantastic!!! Eventually the pumping slows down, and he tells me that's all he can do. He pulls out. That's fine. I'm happy. I'm all fucked out. I roll over onto my side to enjoy my extended pleasures. I'm resting. He staggers out of the bedroom to wash up in the bathroom.

He says I'm his hot wife, and he's a lucky guy. I'm the lucky woman. I don't know many women who get fucked the way I do.

We realize that today is really our celebration of our chocolate anniversary. I was overdue for some major maintenance. That was a super-sized kick-starter session. Only now I realize that we should've been having sex a lot more often, to keep in our best sex shape. Even a couple of week's hiatus from good sex has drastic consequences. But I'm as good as new now. So is he.

Him – You'll be the belle of the parking lot Moms when you pick up the kids.

Me – Can we do this again tomorrow?

Him – I wish.

9 TEXTS

As a small part of our sex life, we text each other. No sexy pictures. Somehow, somewhere, that can be illegal. We prefer putting our thoughts and feelings into words. It's an important part of our sex communication. Our texts let the other person know how we're feeling. They put a nice, warm smile on our faces. They help us get thru the day easier. They also help set the right atmosphere for the next time we're together. Here's a sample of texts from him to me:

- I'm the luckiest guy in the world. Never in a million years did I dream I'd snag such a beautiful, smart, and super sexy girl!!! Thank you for marrying me!!

- I'd like to put your boobs in my mouth.

- Those yoga pants look fantastic!!!

- I went into work today, and realized I was hungry. Hungry for some delicious, juicy, luscious hair pie.

- I want to mouth-fuck you.

- I want to French kiss your pussy – tonight!!!

- You have the best, most stunningly beautiful ass I have ever seen. I can't believe I'm married to such a sexy, gorgeous woman. I'm just dumbfounded when I think about that.

- Thank you, Sweetie, for sticking with me all these years and for being the great love of my life!!

- You're the prettiest, sexiest, most amazing woman I ever set eyes on. I'm incredibly happy to have you.

- I love you!!

- It's an insult to introduce you as just my wife... unless I also say that you are my one and only soul mate and the very great love of my life.

- Want me to eat your hairy pussy? I have a taste for her tonight. Just say the word...

- I love you, Big Tits.

- You know what's nice? Going through life married to your best friend.

- I nominate you for MILF - er, Mom – of the year.

- You have an impeccable ass.

- I wish I was eating your ass right now...

- Wish we were fucking right now.

- I'm going to enjoy you on our vacation!

- I want to lay you on your tummy and fuck you in the ass. From the top of the shaft to the bottom of the penis, I want to plunge it into your ass.

- Today, your ass looked the best I've ever seen!

- Your pant size is "great-ass" size. So, no, you don't need to lose weight.

- There's a great club on the inside, but good luck getting past the bouncer. [In reference to my ass]

- I have an itch relief stick for you. You can come get it any time.

- Your pussy tastes delicious!

- Right smack dab in the chocolate. Nice and messy. Deal?

- Your ass is the best ass ever!!!

- Your butt is BIG, as in PH Phat, as in PH BIG.

- I want to play grab-ass with you.

- I wish I had you back in my mouth right now.

And here's a sample of texts from me to him:

- My ass feels great! Thanks so much for earlier!!!

- Thanks so much for last night!! I had a wonderful time!! Miss you so much!!

- I'm looking forward to seeing you tonight.

- I'm so happy!

- I'm walking around the hotel room right now, wearing only my thong, waiting for you.

- I need to fuck you so bad! Come home!!

- I can't wait till tonight.

- I can't wait till you get home!!

10 THE ALARM CLOCK

I'm looking at my husband, and thinking how nice his dick would fit inside my ass.

Me – When are we gonna fuck?

Him – Oh, I don't know… There's the kids, my work…

Me - I'm your first priority.

Him – Yes, you are.

Me – And I've been very patient lately.

Him – You have?

Me – Yes. And I was wondering when's the next time we're going to fuck? Can we schedule something?

Him – How about the day after tomorrow?

Me – But I'm your first priority. How about today? Tonight!

Him – What do you have in mind?

Me – I was thinking we could have some frontal action, and then some back action.

Him – Yes, when the butt doesn't get any action, then she complains a lot.

Me – Last time she didn't get ANY action, and I can't remember the last time we had sex. It's been that long.

Him – I want to do a nice job for you, and that means taking lots of time. Good things don't happen very fast.

Me – I understand that we have lots of time constraints. I'll be fine with several quickies instead of one marathon session.

Him – We can see what happens. I have a lot on my mind.

Me – Like what?

Him – Like paying off the credit card, like paying for college, like finishing my work for tomorrow. I love to have sex with you, I'm just not in the mood.

Me – Good sex will help everything get better. It'll make you feel years younger. It'll make you look years younger. And it'll make those problems a lot smaller.

Him – Maybe in the morning after I have a good night's sleep.

Me – I'm looking forward to it.

I'm beginning to think that I'm asking for way too much sex way too often. Aren't guys supposed to be the ones constantly on the alert for sex? ANY kind of sex? They're supposed to be the ones begging their wives for sex. For some reason our relationship is all twisted around. Maybe the other couples don't chase each other at all. I guess that's a lot different because we have great sex – the mind-blowing, shining-eyes, type of sex. I don't know what's going on. I know he works a lot. I know he's tired. I know he's a great father. There're some things I just don't understand.

When I have the time to think about spending time with my husband, and don't get any quality time, then I start writing my thoughts down. I guess it fills up the time, and also some sort of need. This kind of time can happen anywhere, and at any time. I just need to have enough downtime available to have my thoughts wander to the pleasures of the flesh. Looks like I'm sleeping tonight. By myself.

It's morning, and I need to start getting ready for the day. I check on the kids in the room down the hall. They're sleeping, so I need to be quiet. I get up, and go take a hot shower. After my shower, I decide to get back into bed with my husband. He's still sleeping. I like having him lay next to me. It's a good feeling. I get under the covers and decide to get back to sleep. I'm tired. My hair's wet, but I could use some extra zzzzz's. My hand wanders over to his side. I realize we're under the same layer of covers. I pet his hip gently. Yes, he's there. Sleeping. He's turned away from me. I plant a gentle kiss on his left shoulder. I like to kiss him because I love him. I move my body over to be next to his body. We're back to back. There's nothing sexual about it. There's full body contact, from our shoulders to our toes. Oh, the toes. My toes start to quietly roam up and down his calves. He stirs. I'm glad he's stirring. Maybe that's the point. Maybe we could get something going before the kids wake up and stop everything. He stirs a little more. He realizes I'm up and laying next to him. He smiles. He's glad I'm here. I like to see that. He turns over so his front is laying alongside my back. His right hand roams over my shoulder, and then over to my stomach. He's going somewhere. I like where he's going. His hand finds my pussy. I smile. My hand finds his dick, and super-gently claw-grabs him repeatedly, until dickie grows. Now I know he's aroused. I ask my husband for a quickie. He says the kids are down the hall, and we'll wake them up. I promise to be quiet. I don't think he believes me, but he can't resist the situation. Hey, I'm horny, and so is he. Priorities tend to get immediately shuffled around sometimes. This is one of those times. We don't want to waste this opportunity. I dough-roll dickie between the palms of my hands. He tells me to get on my tummy. He's going to give me a massage. Oh, I like that idea. I'm wearing a brown velour jacket, grey yoga pants, and a red thong. I turn over on my tummy, and he straddles my legs. He gives my shoulders a quick massage. We really don't have that much time. The kids are worse than an alarm clock. You can shut off an alarm clock. You can't shut off kids. His hands follow down my back. His palms massage the top of my crack. That feels sooooo good! He keeps massaging my crack, and his hands flow down to my cheeks, the back cheeks. I could lay there all day long getting my butt massaged. It's that good of a feeling. He peels down my yoga pants, and sees my red thong.

Him – Now that's a nice site!

I'm so glad he likes it. Red is his favorite color, especially as one of my thongs. I didn't plan it that way, but I'm sure glad it played out that way. He continues massaging my asscheeks. He's getting really heated up. He's laying on top of me, stroking his dick against my ass. How I want his dick to be inside my ass! He lays on top of me. I love to feel him laying on top of me. There's something so sensual about it. A full body smush. He thrusts dickie up and down my crack. How I wish my pants were off! ! His hands shoot underneath me, and grab my boobs, as he's pressing down on me from the top. Did my boobs just harden? I can't tell for sure, but it feels great. He pulls his left hand from underneath me, and grabs a whole lock of my hair. He gently yanks it back. That's really sensual!! If only we were really fucking. Everything else is there. Meanwhile, I'm grabbing with my ass. He must feel my cheeks clamping down on dickie. My ass has internal muscles and external muscles. I'm using the external muscles now. He's so loaded! He tells me he wants to fuck me, but he's not going to. It's those kids again. What a mood killer!! He gets up off the bed, and stands alongside me. He pulls down my yoga pants, and my thong. He asks me to roll over on my back. I oblige. I certainly don't want to argue. Not at this time. Not about this. My knees are up. My legs slowly spread as his fingers find their way between them. He's masturbating my clitoris while having a finger in my ass. That feels soooo good! For some reason I'm interested in pussy sex this morning. The butt stuff feels great, but my itch is up my pussy. He's moving pretty fast, and I love it. I'm so heated up that I can move fast too. I keep hoping he'll enter a finger in my pussy. I keep grabbing with my pussy. I want to grab something. Can he feel that I'm grabbing with my pussy? I'm not sure, but I'm sure that I want something inside my pussy. I want his dick inside of me. But I'll take a finger or two as well.

Ok, I'll request it.

Me – Please put a finger inside me.

Him – OK.

And he does. The finger slides inside of me. I'm sure he feels the heat from inside my body. It's almost too much heat. This gives me the most intoxicating feeling. I feel the finger enter me. I feel every millimeter that it covers, and I relish it. He puts a second finger inside of me. Now there are two fingers inside of me. Two fingers are even better than one.

He pulsates his finger inside my pussy. Oh, that feels so good!! He's reaching for the g-spot knob. He's pressing on it. I can feel myself squirting inside of me. He's pressing on the top of the wall. All of these pleasurable feelings flood my body. Was that a solo pussy, no dick, orgasm? If it was, then it was a small one, a solid one. I keep grabbing with my pussy walls. The grabbing makes the feelings overwhelm my brain with pleasure. I grab over, and over, again. These intense feelings keep flooding my brain, and I love it so much!! I must keep quiet. The kids are in the house. I'm quiet. The feelings keep flooding my brain. I'm having trouble concentrating on my pussy. The next feelings keep overwhelming the previous feelings. Pretty soon I'm living inside my head feeling fantastic. This must be a pussy orgasm. Whatever he's doing is working. I hope he remembers his technique. Eventually the feelings start to waft away from my brain. Unbelievable!!

I turn to him, and grab dickie. I need to do my part. His balls are really full. He needs to cum to get relief, and satisfaction. He's hard, so I keep stroking him with my right hand. He says it feels great even though it's through his thick fleece pajamas. He tells me he's going to cum. I keep on stroking. Suddenly I feel the wetness soaking thru his pants. I realize he came.

So, no lube, no dickie sex, no oral sex. That was a purely clitoral orgasm. I'm surprised. I'm pleased that I'm surprised. I'm also pleased because I'm happy. Whatever he did, worked. I'm very happy for the rest of the day.

ABOUT THE AUTHOR

The author, Tassa DeSalada, is a happily married mother of four kids living in California. Her husband helped her find her sexuality after having lost it due to her numerous pregnancies. Together they developed their sex lives to a point way past where they were pre-pregnancy. She is currently writing a series of books called "The Chocolate Arts Project".

CPSIA information can be obtained
at www.ICGtesting.com
Printed in the USA
LVHW012009281118
598528LV00027B/734/P